The Steel Garden

Lorna J. Waite

WP
BOOKS

Published by Word Power Books 2011
43-45 West Nicolson Street
Edinburgh EH8 9DB
www.word-power.co.uk

Printed and bound in Scotland.
Designed by Andy Rice

British Library Cataloguing in Publication Data.
A catalogue record for this book is available from
the British Library.

ISBN 978-0-9566283-4-3

The publisher acknowledges financial support from
W. and J. Knox Ltd., Kilbirnie, towards the publication
of this volume.

Dedicated with love to the memory of my uncle, Jackie Boyd and in honour of my friends Frank Hynd and Barry Thompson and all my ancestors who worked at Glengarnock Steelworks.

Lorna J. Waite was born and brought up in the shadow of Glengarnock Steelworks in the town of Kilbirnie, Ayrshire.

She was educated at Garnock Academy and the University of Edinburgh and has recently completed a Ph.D. at the University of Dundee. She is a Fellow of the Society of Antiquaries of Scotland and a Gaelic learner.

She has written on the visual arts for a wide range of publications and was associate editor of Variant. She has worked as an arts co-ordinator, support worker, adult education tutor and lecturer with a broad range of community groups and organisations. A constant has been the commitment to increasing access to education and the arts for those whose voices go unheard.

Her poems have featured in 100 Favourite Scottish Football Poems, Bella Caledonia and Poetry Scotland. The Steel Garden is her first collection of poetry.

The Steel Garden

Shift Change

Where are the words o my steel imagination?
Fettle
Bloom
Tap
Teem

Whaur did they take the lost furnace?
Whit wir their names, they aa had names?
Men intimate wi their temperament
Ca'd tae name their world.

Are there shiftin teams o steelworkers
Oan the shores of Slag Hill
Waitin to be remembered
Am I the only wan who
Sees the land like this?

The eye o the furnace teems metal through my veins
A woman o Hephaestos, my bones are metal,
Winged feet an golden shoes
I emerge fae the oozy clay o the sunny neuk
Valley born wi an upturned eye
A made-self creation myth
Withoot god.
Enchanted wi the rhythm o the workers
Tackety boots tip-toe early mornin shift change,
A dense whirl o noise seepin through
Thin walls o council houses.
We hear everythin, nae acoustic secrets
In the auld hoose, nightshift rolls,
The early risin o the baker, the first meal fur the weans
Breaks the seal o the day I have dreamt amang the stars.
While the furnace charges, swellin wi the night
Like the woman's battered face, a discharge o energy
Fae the wrath o the domestic god
Ares unleashed in the livin room o blame.

Make me a jewel for peace in yer forge, Hephaestos,
Forsake the arms o the gods for they bear nae wounds,
Rest yer foot in the palm o my hand
Dress the women in garments
O bejewelled finery, sheer as lace, strong as steel,
A workin class glamour o Blastie myth.

First Hands

My hands, once feather-heavy wi pain
Caress keyboard wi pain-free flight
Heave the weight o burdens in the turnaroon o the heart,
Spin in a whirlygig o dance
Catch fallen stars on secret paths o childhood streets,
Strum strings o unspoken music
Absorb the shock o grief wi upturned palm,
Iron oot those ancient creases in the moon-skin o life
A steel sea o tranquillity in the heart-line o muscle.

First hand knowledge forgives
Fingers yield
Tae language fated in belongin.

The Sentence of a Body

My body is a sentence, the crown o my head
Vibrates wi nouns monumental.
The epiphany o history's drum roll,
Imagination, Outsight, Justice …
Trinity o concepts behind the eyes
Concealin motives, ye disguise shame.

The antennae of the womb huv blood red tentacles
Moon-timed cycles o makin.
An imperturbable centre o desire,
Nervous endins the regular verbs o possibility
A core grammar o loss, a fragment o history
In flesh an metal shard,
Oor memory a cleared condition,
Destruction for your own good.

A prison o the mind, asked tae destroy
Yer ain history, brick by brick -
Folk memory tells the story,
The steelworker oan his final shift,
The last job, the execution o the demolition
Dying ootside the gates o the work.

A Lament for Red Frank

Oor cradle o oor deid
Lies in the lee o oor hame grun
Castin a protective shadow wi the risin sun
Ye will hear the chantin
O a fortnightly chorus of belongin
The dead like to be sung to
The dead like to be praised in the voices o the people
The dead like to be thought o, as wi us, withoot sorrow.

This is the Buddhist way
The dead lead us tae love
Like a child's drawin o the field o green
Coloured in, nae grey shadows
Black granite headstones are
Outside defenders on the cemetery wall
Hae comrades an common ties
In the children's drawins o the deid.

I sing you Burns, Frank, and swear I feel ye
Rustle underground wi relief
Somebody remembered tae sing !
I sing tae maself beside yer grave
You are immense in my mind,
Your heart so big it left a rent in me
I cover ower with finest Ayrshire lace
Delicate, fragile, woven fae women's hands
As light as your kindness, daisies yer favourite
I embroider on the main chamber o my heart
I sing to you Frank the story of us,
Are ye listenin to the wee lassie who loved ye?

You are monumental like steel, the man o sociable heart
The skies teemed ingots of rain when we lowered ye doon
My tears heavier, a torrent of grief
At this unbearable sight,
You, a deep wound.
Our work unfinished, so much tae dae -
Ye radiated a furnace o love for me

Tellt me to forgive that day
Gripped by a desperate desire for praise and truth
Untellt stories mended in the mind
Old worn pictures o sufferin shot through wi a light
Always in yer eye.

We are a' lost, yer chair bides empty
Unfilled, still yearning for ye -
The brothers are all there,
Eddie, Bobby, the two Jims, Jack, Ian, George.
Pain kept in, dreams untravelled
Bring a distance tae the faces o yer friends -
Our silent look away
For whit is there tae say?
You are visited by us a'
Kept in flowers, mine ayewis yellow an red
Team colours an the hue o yer hair
Buddhist colours, peaceful like.

The book o us, Frank, is writin
Yer heart's presence in the kindness o hands
Words to suggest the poetry an steel in the marrow o yer bones,
Fed on the seaweed-tinged taste o the Ayrshire coast
Watered by the Garnock,
It was you who tried to rescue our Goddess fae the burn
The river in spate, a missin chalice, a broken arm
Hygieia smiles on her benevolent suitor.
Oh man o steel I sit beside oor loch
Weep for the absent space, the forgotten place
Your loss has left me adrift,
Licking salt fae my lips,
The waves of oor loch are calm an gentle,
Reflect the full moon of yer luminous smile.

Burns wiz in ye, Frank, oor cherished poet
The love-bind o Ayrshire folk,
For we are The Inventory, the red-wud Kilbirnie Blasties
O the steel work, the mills an the rollin o the last bloom.
The flowers o yer grave are tended by women
My sister visits often, my niece so young, is wise,
"Frank was a good man", she says.
I offer ye my voice

Sing words of love -
Ach, ye wid laugh at the sight,
The site where I speak to you for advice
Close to where we were forged.
Amidst furnaces and the wimplin weariness o oor history's silence
What do you say tae the woman who loved ye,
No the young lass when your hair was red -
The woman of your grey-haired time
Has a heart that blooms wi every utterance o yer name.

I mind -
My ancestors in the flowerin of yer life
Weave a pattern of memory in lace
Wi mountain daisies an red roses
The yellow an red o oor country's soul
Stitches are the healin threads o woman's words.

James with the Ancestors who Shine

(in memory of Barry Thompson and in honour of James Thompson)

In the museum o ancestral life
Are many brothers who sang -
They are but distant echoes now
Swirlin in a constellation o stars
The Star o' Rabbie Burns
Glorious song o moonlight remembrance
Stars ayewis evoke oor deid
An eternal twinklin o skinklin memory
So seductive tae the mournin, the visible eternal
Laws o physics can be holy contradictory
A consolation tae the infinity o death.
Embrace the moondust o thought
Dinnae worry ower the lost years
Names are important in the mournin maps o the sky -
I have a place for the brothers in ma universe
Childhood helpers heal the ruptures o history.

Venus shows herself the night
Accompanyin sister Moon,
The bow an arrow of fated life
Reflector of memory, when she smiles wi me
Under her, at the motherless mountain -
I remember you aa' clearly
In the enigma of solitude, I dream
Of the Dead, promise the earth a kiss,
Touch your archive wi hands of wonder
Musky reliquary o dreamed imaginin
The physical marrow o yer reality
Is in the recovery of image and the sound touch o your words,
" I rescued them fae the rubbish bin, they were goin tae put them oot."

The working class memory keeper has dirty hands an a furtive gaze
You are tradition bearer an stealthy archivist
 In the sideboard drawers o a council hoose
The tap o a wardrobe in a bedroom protectin history
In the vigilant eyes o the keeper o belongin
In the rags and bones, the watcher of the found fragments
Keeps faith wi the young until death.

You are now the star o yer ancestor's song -
Yer brother has been accorded his rightfu place
Yer light is sung in the pages o my thought
In the language o praise, ye are the holders o knowledge
O song an story, picture an path
Ransackin the containers o clearing,
Retrievin oor history tae make it shine.

Sons of Hephaestos

Sons o Hephaestos, I remember you a'
Honourable metalworkers o a mythless age
Ye cast fae clay the mould o livelihood
Hewed rock fae earth in mines an quarries
Of oor Ayrshire frontier
An artery of stane frozen in the name o Thatcher
Disnae pulse wi life, immovable nursing o wrath
Have sympathy for my vengeance,
Tragic for the peace woman, naturally.

Still my heart beats in tune tae the pulse o the furnace
The accumulation o a pour oot o steely grief
I will discharge the liquid metal o my soul
Oan land rusted wi the antipathy o yer politics.

Were ye jealous o our love for each other?
Unbendin humour an historic strength
Oor workin class joie de vivre unkent
In the austere gaze o your blinded sight?
Iron ladies of the forge of Hephaestos
Looked upon the sacred smith
Bejewelled an radiant wi the gleam o metallic beauty,
An industry o myth died, reborn wi vision
The tales o the Steel Woman listened tae
In the embers o a fire, nae angel of history can smoor.

Artemis and the Archives
of the Ancestors of Metal

Begin in the place where they may be thocht tae be found

The forensic scent o dusty papers
In the archive o the hunt
Haunts a nocturnal imagination o moonlit proof
Evidence o materiality required
Do I exist in yer history?

"Aye, noo whit was there in Kilbirnie then?", the removal man asked,
Flittin here from place tae place, among the flooded Kilbirnie race
A Burns melodrama o motion in space.
"The steelwork and the mills", I state
Empty places in history, he didnae ken
Name, location, oor sheer steely magnificence,
A skyscape of proud furnace, the cathedral o early mind
Ayewis, the harmonic simplicity o form.

Ye played your illicit game
An unfolding inferiorism
In the tempest of your reign,
This Macgregor will always have his name
As head of house in the corridor of class-hating power
Subaltern Scots pass through the obedience threshold.

We hunted wi dogs on the site ye ken
Wild rabbit an ironworks village
A kestrel made her hame in the
Steel buttress o the rolling mill
Artemis calls her hounds tae heel
On the shore o the cleared place.

But First Hear My Muse

Go on huntress into sharp edges o time
Roll back an unfold
The event structure o memory
Scar tissue as strong as fate
The sheer bloody pain of it all

Unfelt in the boarding school
Banking lands o share protection,
New plants do not grow
The meek are no meant to inherit the earth after all
In yer colonial ministry of energy,
We became dispersed an displaced.

I hunt you doon in the abandoned mill
In the destroyed archive, in the minutiae of yer omissions
In yer telling of the story in yer ain words no mine
In the nocturnal visits to oor place
Ancestor hame of the Raws,
The Waites, tap o the list in the MacFarland namin,
I ken the answer wi evidence fae the people
How heroic amidst the breakin and crackin o metal, toon an
meanin
For ye see, education works in the Blastie mind o the Burns loving
folk
Techniques o true oppression dinnae fettle my readin o yer tellin.

Begin in the place where yer story is tae be heard -
Whaur dae ye hear the voices o yer people?
Do you ken their names?
Initiation tae the wild mind o the hunter beside the moonlit loch
He was my ancestor ye ken, Charlie Waite
Feedin weans rabbit fae the land, rollin metal,
Furnace eye, Slag Hill metal water
An night vision Blastie soul o the ironworker lad.

John MacFarland's lantern is the story
O the illuminated names o ancestors
Written in compassionate moonlight
Sensed still among rose bay willow herb
Generatin itself amidst the rubble o industry
An architecture o plantation an underground contamination
Weighs heavy in my steel-armoured memory
A tideline o toxicity willnae forgive ye
The blackband ironstone o my body holds thegither
A bridge o metal tongue, an underground archway o restless flight,
Furnaces shaped like beehives, a womb o steel,
Liquid hot an fiery with fertility.
Didn't Hephaestos the smith God love Aphrodite after a?

Artemis has hunted doon the Destroyer of the smith-god
Rests happily oan Slag Hill, sleepin dogs lie -
Athena honours Hygeia in action
Aphrodite whispers the sangs o the folk.

End in the place whaur they are loved

Ben Ledi

The prepositions have meaning unseen
On in at with me Gaelic understands
Our specific fluid elemental soul
My soundscape of senses
Feels your sympathy with my belonging
Accepts the work of my feet and
Breath always receptive to love.

I know where the old ones danced
Your skirts and pleats in full flowing summer flounce
Flourish amidst wild step and red rampant sunset
On your glorious and green high land expanse
With sex and flower, inviting and warm flesh of light
The body wishes to be seen like you
Open and desirous, so freely vulgar with beauty
I know this from the song of you.

I saw the bowed heads of buttercups
Forego prayer to dance a golden reel
With the windy sun trails of your spring dance
I saw the dignity of my town in tender stalk
Upright and gallus in the wind, the delicate flower
Of farm roads and football field
Unyielding to violent wind, resilient sanctuaries
Of courage not yellowing with age
Childhood magic under the chin foretelling
The tined fortune of the last steel bloom.

Crannog and Canoe

You held me today
Offered your guides of flight
To future wayward direction
Hid your best clothes for another time
Fresh, waiting, streaked lines of piebald skin
An intense blur of deep green fern
Of inheld fecundity, waiting.

A quick stop before the cycle begins
I am in step, bleeding
Coming out of winter's harsh terrain
Crawling on your skin like a newborn child
Silent, I see your submerged history
Trace line under water of crannog and settlement.

Reciting my lines
I ache for your wiggle and turns
The final joke, you laugh at me benevolently -
I always fall for your false summit
Charming, gullible, is this it?
Out of mist, a new contour of difficulty
An intense mirage.

You go easy on me today
Skin on skin,
Tongue over lip, foot on earth
Water and blood meeting -
The ravens check my way
Choose rocks of significance.
They know the song I walk to sing -
Of Kilbirnie Loch, the iron slag
Artefacts of old belonging
-Crannog, canoe, a lion ewer-
An indigenous trinity of invisible objects
Revealing the site of the mark of memory
Erased, I see the homeopathic structure
Ben Ledi looks down upon the fluttering flag
The Lion Rampant flies over Lubnaig's
Submerged hearths.

Our water rests quietly
Off the leisure trail, of no cultural import
Treasures hoarded by the gatekeepers of capital
The city holds the local in cupboards
Unseen by curious eyes
The heron flies at halfmast over the loch
In early morning reverie
I stand upon a moon platform of shining slag
Pour fresh water from the missing chalice of Hygieia
Glide like the swan over Blastie water
Close to the sacred, no flags mark ownership.

Water, Memory

After five years of watching me
Trace worn-out lines of movement
On a Lewis hillside, Agnes told me kindly,
" The beach likes to be visited by you ".

I follow the tracks of the feet of children
Permitted now to say Madainn Mhath
Without punishment, language wriggles free
An oxygen of vocabulary in harmless air
Breathe free speech on the path of belonging.

On the daily ritual to the return of the waves
Their surging entrance to the beach of drama
Drunken crashing beside companion stone
Lapping entry to the shape-shifting sand
Where love was formed, water washes up my tide of souls.

The Cemetery and the Loch

Our cemetery likes to be visited by us
Our ain well-tended garden of the remembered
The bones of our ancestors cradled
By red brick wall and cast iron railing,
An industrial place
Frequent shifts of Blastie folk
Reside close to where the work was,
Water lapping the shores of our dead
In a history out of sight
The Celtic monks saw
Our water was sacred
Cells of beehive knowledge built
Close to Kilbirnie Loch
Imagined devices for worship still remain
Ornate carvings reveal territory
Intangible ancient groves hide
Under the cloored stane of the Auld Kirk.

The skin shoreline of my body
Ripples and shimmers with a wink to the west,
Here, my Ayrshire heart hears kinship
With oystercatcher, sandpiper and seal
Dancing on borders, resting on tidelines
My coastal soul is loyal to water.
My body remembers our loch from all points north
She welcomes me with daybreath,
Furtive moonlight, on well trodden footsteps
Echoes of clanking parts and whisper of worker.
Her dignity remains intact, offers hospitality,
sacred and dark, to the ancestor of the Gael.
"She likes to be visited by me …", she tells,
I scatter seeds of wild flowers in honour
Of the lost metal world.

British Steel Blues

A well-meaning Corus of indifference
Greets my eager eyes,
Well- recorded notes of destruction
Produce evidence of the journey's futility.

I thought I would come hame
By going far away, recreate the landscaped mind,
A silhouette of steel on the valley horizon
From the hill ridge, the view sees me looking,
Smiles in homeopathic compassion
She is not us, sadly.

The red dragon sun lifts the opaque veil
From the Welsh valley, spires of furnace appear
Industrial cathedrals, not a place for forgetting,
Steel travels up the water, stripped bare,
Sent into exile, the barbed wire destiny
Of exported protection.
Our archives came here, nationalised,
Ownership of the Scottish people surely?
"I can show you where we put them before destruction,"
He proudly states.

The British corporation has been thorough
In the inventory of lost documents, it is noted
'Rescued from a rubbish tip…Destroyed'.
The steel chamber of history stinks
With the alchemy of waste,
We have become…recycled, fit for toilet and kitchen,
A sanitised domestic removal.
The multinational profit of Kimberley Clark
Sustained by the erasure of the records of culture
A private commodity of storage, a unit of profit,
Dispatch efficiently the cleared history
Of Merry and Cunningham, the early days,
The origin myth of my town,
Metal is in us.

Colville's civic pride and company store
Seals of authentic naming, wiped clean.

Sent to the Welsh repository
-So British, the diffusion of responsibility -
The Celts injure the archive with obedience,
A subaltern history far apart from dream of state
Our homeless nations load trucks of memory
Disperse our goods to the cleared lands
Do the dirty work of others,
Asset strip and wipe your tears upon tissue of empire
The paper hankie may be the touch of the past
Upon my cheek, a reincarnation of sorts.

The Secrets of Hygieia

Hygieia waited for me to drink from her missing chalice
Caress the folds of her skirt with tender touch -
Women of Kilbirnie, the goddess is on your way
Do you not see her weeping for the empty streets?

The abandonment of health denounces her name
Without prejudice, crown her with careful touching
Of her wound, her emptiness is our prosthetic
Replacement for ourselves.

His Final Tap

In the time of hidden wounds and private grief
It was not customary to lay flowers
At the public place of the fallen one.
Now, greylag goose clouds chase the day away
Pink beaks of setting light poke the surface water
A heartspun hue appears with the waning sun
I wait for the water to answer my question -
Where exactly did he die?

Was it near the regulated recovery trees?
The planted, stunted sentinels grow sparse
Cover over the mise- en- scene.
Or in the grassy meadow, left to
Bury its emptiness with dignity?
No ritual was attended to,
You are unmarked by stone, symbolic tree or
Polythene supermarket foliage flowers.
I imagine you in the forget-me-not
Beside the water-outlet for the work,
In the voice of the oystercatcher, "Be wise".

You died on the same date
As the Glencoe massacre -
The fingerless pain of bone-chilled women,
Bloodied feet streaking the terrain across rock and water
To the magic of the white stone
And the MacIntyre friend with healing hands -
My fearful flight across Ayrshire field and road
Lingers in flashback,
Women run from danger, the death of history.

A steelworker knocks on the door of the old house,
In the time before the birds rise,
In the gloom of winter's morning shift
The sound is hesitant and unexpected
A chain of broken words and love -
Dead.

My mother's scream echoes off the walls
Spiralling up like toxic gas
Till I choke on breathless fear
Rescue fantasies fed by the movement
Of feet on pedal, towards your safe house
I no longer have a destination.

We have reached our end-point, you and I
Before our love blossomed as story.
Elemental and tragic like the steel
Extracting the measure of you
With its temperamental, metal-minded
Blood charging of the heart
Straining to bear
The weight of your final tap.

Clearing the Raws

Do we all travel to the loch and remember Heraclitus?
Change is change and all changes
With the revolution of revelation, take heart.
The bird will sing for you on sparse branch, even
If only rosebay willow herb greens the toxic land,
Shards of pink blooms lessen the wound.

We cannot see the lost houses
I have found here the village of silence
This discontent with your treatment
Finds me placing the debris
Of others pleasure in black bags
-Making you tidy for your show to me -
Stains of human history gnaw the earth
Folk dream amidst the litter of mourning
And the chatter of bitterness.

A harsh wind bites the water,
Snarling shapes remind me
Of our unspoken-ness
My voice is out, speaking here
Reconciling myself to invisibility
Under young birch, I cultivate strategy,
The moon rises over the armaments depot
The sacred well is concealed, the saints are quiet
Hidden by underground bunkers storing death's rhizomes.

On Looking at a Drawing of the Raws

A culture without a camera drew itself -
Simple graphite marks outline the imagination of home,
Name the streets now razed over, redefined -
Neither idealisation nor humility are present
In remembering the ironworks village.

The Raws were in them,
The furnaces, close as a baby's breath,
Lithuanian blinis and Ulster linen
On scarred box bed, echo of emptiness thrives
In your unfed heart, overcrowding breeds
Reluctance to touch violence, unyielding to tears.

Poetic Proof
(An Empirical Act)

I will make solid in the tactile,
Common Sense philosophical way
The limits of your evidence against me -
What case is there to answer?
Does the land ask questions in its insistence
Upon the nature of Nature, a natural event?
Unyielding is the Biblical flood of blame -
Heed the warning, the trumpet sounded
In the political sign of the protesters' song.

... on the march, the placard was bigger than me...
DON"T LET GLENGARNOCK BECOME A GHOST TOWN
Walking with adults, too scared to ask, "What is a ghost town? "
I rode the yearly train at Beith, funfair ghosts feart and trembling,
Glad-eyed stare at the boundless rush,
The erotic thrust of the safety of fear
Speed and scale amplify the thrills of memory
Time rails in the missiles of hurt,
Raining with fallout on the bruises of children.

The waveforms of trauma are strangers
With no recollected warning, flashbacks flare,
Phosphorous white, hide and heat seek the furnace,
Take up residence in the rubble where they came to knock ye down.
Did ye look at the gasping breath, the anxious arms of steelworkers,
Crumbling under the deadbeat factory, covering up history
In the underground chambers of unrolled blooms?

In the making of them is a heartless cruelty,
Bitterness festers in the No Mother schools of the Elite -
In punishing the poor lack of empathy a sign
Of psychopathy, ye know -
Did you learn to kill well?
Can the poet of the land speak with the truth?
Of the social scientist, "Ye were all mad!"
What did Freud teach ye, young thinker

Of the unease in your culture?
The land fractures with the held hate of many flags,
Are we together under a blue and white shelter?
A political song sings of fresh anger
... An inhale of determined breath..
The slow exhale of the democratic quest
Call it a bracelet of light, charmed by the wearing
And touch of hand on society's skin.
Freud and Adam Ferguson knew this,
From muscle memory, the indivisible structure
Of the whole fluid mutuality, a Scottish Zen
Of sympathy, metaphysical proof
Of the poetic method.

The heartless Union is devoid of fruit,
Waiting seeds of hope twist new mind,
Cyclic winds of change howl in Scotland
Rage and spill and churn and blow over
Newly planted trees, wearing silk ribbons -
This is how the Gaels remember, after all.
Smile at the sound on a light-kissed shore,
The blood red of woman wraps the liberty tree
Burns bloomed in the Masonic club of youth,
Beside the burn of memory is the classroom
Nearby, Coila protects the republic of self.

The Health of the Street is Critical

The work of the hands of the mothers
Rests in the red brick and cast iron gate
Of the dyework demolition death.
Did ye think of the winders when ye unravelled
Our relationship of water, land and people?

The offices of the elected remain standing -
The goddess looks askance,
Classical ruins of humbling ideology
Ache behind the cracked stone walls
Of the crumbling town hall.

The public health of the street remains critical
Fractures untended like a neglected child,
Arteries blocked with the funnel of corrosion
Vernacular stone crumbles
Under the sledge hammer of history.
The flat planes of the Tesco car park
Offer no comfort to equality's eyes.

Where is the rest for the contemplation of flowers?
The power of water, surely, may live a new dream?
Is the river speaking, angry wave
Upon wave of destroyed brick piled high
On the untended texture of the land?
The children of the Milton scheme
No longer cross the great burn of playful imagination
Gated off rights of way permit no adventure
Behind cleared orchard and fenced woodland path.
Whispers of a ghost, the White Lady of Redheugh
Peering through branches unseen by adult eyes
I looked for her under chestnut trees,
Imagined supernatural protection, reality dimmed,
The poet found solitude there, secret and safe,
Children are blind now to this mystery.
Along the old trail, new doors and few openings -
No access to conquered wisdom
Chestnuts do not shine

In the curious hands of the children
Polishing dreams found at their feet.
The burglar alarms of night vision
Blind the cataract eyes of the fearful
The builder has trespassed against us.

Steel Myths and Glass Vision

In the box of glass memory
Inside the library of lost childhood
The goddess of the books entrusts me,
Guardian of the early mind
With the saved artefacts of our myth
In these slides of our steelmaking
I see continents of history and refracted metal gods.

We could plunder the myths
For our own inherited satisfaction
Find solace in the ancient stories of iron.

Hera chucked her wean out of paradise
Poor Hephaestos, despite a bad start,
Made beauty and married love.
Maybe, our ancestors held this mythic tale,
Powerful were the sons of Vulcan,
I prefer Hephaestos, more philosophical.
The woman of the water were kind to him,
He would have worked well
Beside you all, the red wud blasties,
I would have been welcome at the smithy
Maybe, it is Aphrodite who tells the honest tale
Driven by love, such trouble she is,
Hanging about the Big Linn, at closing time,
Down by the auld network, of all places.

I encounter Siderite, iron goddess
Falling to earth in meteoric curve,
Our furnaces, emerging from the land
Explosive and powerful, creative origin noise,
Extraction of stone to metal
The energy and spirit of fire
The blasted heat of the furnace -
The Cyclops were his pals,
The smithy held vision in the eye.

Walk into the Narrative
Holding Hands with History

The god of the furnace found fame
Safe in the land of the well mothered,
Mount Etna was kind to the hard worker
The industrious ones took up residence close by.

Hera, unforgiving wordless mother,
Motherless other, she was hard to please,
Where is the story of her absence?
Mother the motherless, Athena,
Hephaestos shone for you.

Tobar Na Mhathair, mother well,
Such a fine name, ancient instruction
And Etna forgotten.
Well is the mother of memory
Deep plunging into that water womb
Of unbearable pain, running in fear
From an invisible wound.

Hephaestos was fostered by the sea
Thetis and Eurynome, mothers of all things,
Watery and ever circling, a coastal compassion
They weep at the fiery reactor of the nuclear dream,
Radiation is not welcome in the underworld
Of geologic myth.
Goldenberry Hill casts a watchful eye
Over Hunterston.
Like Hera, approval is not imminent.

Hephaestos was brave,
Returned to the place of violence
And made things anew.
Enter its heart, you belong in the naming,
Tell tales in the making
Make children from the lost words
Of strange night whispers, filter memory

Pass through a valley of darkness
Poverty lit by candles of weary souls
Waiting to hear you speak their name.

Dusty is the archive of the unconscious
Cleaning dirty playing moving against
The weft of a reality unchecked -
(Walter Benjamin understood)
You marked the site where the memory was
Told, excavated and revealed.

The conscience of the children was silent
No-one listened to our chorus of confused words
The language was not known, how to say it
The suffering of the words, poor motherless words
Of unspoken redemption.

Years of cluttering subconscious mind
Stomach ache blues of violent verbs
Insomnia of rightness of the act
The placement of the body sentence
Where heart touches a mirror
Foggy with delusion, aching for belonging
Read my words, suffer little children.
Protect from harm those heroic little ones,
Born from the head of the women of Etna
…..waiting just waiting….stories of resistance
To walk into the narrative holding hands with history.

Classical Kilbirnie

No-one asked the Blastie young,
About the destruction of Steeltown
We sons and daughters of Hephaestos
Are just an old, classic story after all.
Did you know, we too, like the ploughman poet
-Our own, by the way -
Received a fine classical education
Myth is alive in the minds of the young scholars.

Our teacher of Greek and Latin,
Linguist, walker, lover of Scotland
Journeyed to the islands of our soul
Sailed like Odysseus to far off places
Rum, Eigg, Muck.
Are they like Millport? The Sicily of the local mind
Or Rothesay, comparable to Crete, surely
Crowned with working class achievement
Clever girls, we sailed far with language and myth
Athena was proud of her novice storytellers.
I walk past her womenfolk
On the main street of my hometown,
The goddess watches.

From a croft window in Tarskavaig,
First sight of an archipelago
Pebble-sized through the perspective
Of a glass memory, three islands, a trinity of names
Between education and vision, a solitary journey of years.

A history quest for Scotland seeds in the classroom
Of Greek grammar, classical myth and female intelligence,
Thanks you inwardly when the structure of Gaelic
The new language for my own tongue, cracks open
Complexity of speech found in the categories
Of knowledge taught by the local teacher
Like Brendan, she navigates across
The footsteps of the Fianna women.

On Slag Hill: Make New Plans for the Loved Land

On Slag Hill
Stains of iron rust the bank of the loch
In resigned geologic neglect
Manganese, iron ore, sulphur
A waste tip of memory.

I stand on the metal of the fathers
The workers of the furnace rolled steel
See the teardrops of the last tap -
In the steeltown all is quiet now
Still the sound of metal on land
The swans keep faith with water
The oystercatcher in early morning
Reverie sounds the Blastie call to wisdom.

Fishing lines and half moon tents
Lace the shoreline in graceful wave
Hands no longer grasp the tap hole
Rivers of metal run through
The veins of the black iron land
Men sit and contemplate
The stir of surface meaning
The counter balance of history
May tip in our favour
A metronome of history's rhythm
Power of metal and the knowledge of the hunter -
Did the crannog people worship the land?
Gaze at the moon in water-fringed liquid splendour
Make metal here too?
Have food at their favourite spot.

Specular light, like the eye of the furnace
He struggled to open the closed taphole
Teeming was a hard job, double shift toughness
"Too clever to work there, a gentleman",
They all say in recollected telling.

On Slag Hill, iron tears run rivers through my face
Craters of metal moon pit the surface in grief
Tell tales of lost faith, the injured bodyland
A collective trauma of sorts,
The wise doctor would intone.
Still felt keenly in throat
A choking of voice strangled
By removal of the chords of history
We still sing our song
An elegant refrain of friendship
Nameless Blasties wi the steelwork blues
Breathe the air of the bird
Make new plans for the loved land
She is in us all, bear her wound
Extract seeds and fruit of story from the relics.

For ye see, he died there.
My reliquary is the rusting pipe,
Slag glass, fossil black, glistens
From the landfill of rubble, an ancient world
Of crustacean and industrial architecture of stone,
Lies waiting to be seen… shining.
Through the empathy eyes of the giver
The smith-god had helpers.
Golden women with wheels of steel
My hair streaks the wind in blonde wisps
Like kite tails flying over land
Keeping company with the dead ones
Resurrecting your memory
Emboldened by love
This spirit holds death close to water
Consoles the night-time wanderers.

Ancestor Movement Trails 1

Inverness To Kilbirnie: Northeast to Southwest

Your world is in my hands now
Woodturning highland great-grandfather -
I know the Gaelic for wood
I turn spirals into words
Your journey to the south-facing valley
I remember sitting beside the River Ness.

Our branch line of bastards flows to the sea
The poet beside me understands
The exile of the ancestors, the boldness of the traveller,
The necessity of the movement trail,
Stilling the shame of repeated circumstances.

Bastard weans travel far fae shame
Dinnae hing aboot the toon
Waiting for judgement
The tracks of your journey
Cover the trail of the metal
Shifting compass of work
Your highland exile
A respite from whispers
And denied legacy.

You are in her, my mother
The historical repeat
Of the same story
The shame of yer ain kin
Merciless in its pursuit
Of your tolerance
Unforgiving banishment of the unmarried woman
…another same old story for the goddess…
To thole in exile the patriarch of old -
No sympathy for the erotic exploration
Of the body as a journey
Unmoved by admonitions of biblical purity
Women know this to be true

In their monthly return to themselves,
The ebb and flow of desire
A natural relationship.
A journey south
Washes you up on the Ayrshire coast
With receding tidal family ties, there is no anchor.

You have carried with you
The world in a wooden ball
Your woodturner's apprentice piece
From your highland north
Travelled in remembrance
Of young hands at the lathe,
Carving spirals and whirls
Turning tree into toy,
Crafting a smugglers compartment
Wi totey spinning top, made for wee hands,
In the delight of your boyhood.

The terminal moraine of shame
Is no more within me, it has ended -
The childless mother speaks up
For the motherless daughter.
The Gaelic learner retrieves
Further losses and is angered
By the silence of language holders.
In the womb of the writer I will not
Tolerate this moral void.

At the heart of your world
The carved wooden ball sings
Of the joy of making,
A globe of contemplation pocket-sized
To fit the highlander in exile.

I am the custodian of your past
Shame-free and lucid
Shaped by wood, dictionary
And the relics of your craft,
The family object of veneration
Entrusted to the writer -
The branchline of daughters
Has reached the tideline of transmission.
Turning the language of fate
In our own hands, we remember.

Ancestor Movement Trails 2

Glengarnock to New York and Back Again

A mythic transatlantic voyage
Smothered in Scottish pride and fatherless fantasy,
Your mother had an escape plan with guts.
The sea does not pass judgement
The crossing of redemption conceived
In the shadow of the ironworks village.

You were the returner, cast aside,
Excluded from the patriarchal culture
Of the other immigrant men -
A classical mix of Scots and Greek
Ensured your odyssey across
The herring pond of heroic solitude -
The boy sent back hame, five years old,
Motherless on a returning ship
Too young to be considered an exile
The foster care of the stranger
Helped you to overcome bitterness
On the sea, compassion was given.

You never forgot the kindness of emergency,
The holding of your fear by the pity of the poor
This rich vein of care teemed out of you,
A lava flow of love, radiant in the eye
The eye of the furnace is God, so they say -
The glint of your eye on seeing me
Enough to forge a lifetime of devotion
To the blooming of your memory.
In the meeting of our eyes, soul bonds rolled
Out the trajectory of time,
Grief is timeless, we merely cast our loss a form
To make room for the immobility of absence.

My ocean of tears has not stopped,
The love of you has not diminished,
The steelworker in you has not rusted with dereliction
Your grave is loved, an anchor to ourselves.
Evergreen grows wild beside your resting place,
New growth through mourning and the erosion of granite
A stone's throw from the work.

You had an industrial death, classical and Scottish,
Overworked heart and man of dreams,
Odysseus did not return -
You died hoping, heroic in your efforts,
The burden of metal and ship upon you.

Ancestor Movement Trails 3

Scotland to Shotton, Wales.

I went far in search of traditional knowledge
Of the industrial worker, traversed motorways
Through the occupying power
To the land of the other Celtic minority
I gained entry,
In search of the nationalised records
Of Scottish working class history.

Capital trails of corporate lands
Moved by the riches of the selfish
The ownership of history by the shareholder
Of the archive, surely though, we paid for this national record?
Of worthy labour in heroic tonnes of metal
Of profit rolled across imperial continents
Bearing your inscribed name, Glengarnock,
Across arid deserts to hopeful extractive oases of colonial riches.

Now, the repository belongs to the private company
Caretakers of memory appointed by others
The hard hat of the archive keeper belongs
To the building site of history, here the library of records
Will be systematically destroyed far away from home.

"Recycled though", the Corus man states, "nothing wasted,"
Proudly shows me the container for the departing
Documents of history, to be loaded and transported,
Shredded and utilised for socially useful purposes
Like cleaning shit or wiping away the stains
Of historical shame, denying my place in your scheme,
A lesson from the wars of history
Found in the sterile storage shed of a Welsh steeltown,
Far from Glengarnock's shore.

The academic shivers in outrage
At the unnecessary clearance of my history
Authorised for death by others.
 -The security man asks to see my clearance -
No irony intended, seemingly,
Like all feral rebels, I have found the natural way in,
Without surveillance, I crossed the threshold.

Ancestor Movement Trails 4

Naming The Work Map

Siberia
Dummy Lane
Billy Ruffian
Corn Park
Wee Tunnel
Hannah's Farm
Big Tunnel
The Orchard
The Reading Room
The Gas Producers
The Settling Pond
The Raws
The Long Row
Jock's Corner
The Store Place
The Herrin Pond
The Soaking Bay

The shop of melting names
The empty cupboard of genealogies
The order book of the ones who went before
The rolling floor of the mill of metal
The ballroom of steel
The pageant of the Blasties
The arch of memory
The volcanoes of Etna and the Bay of Soaking
The loch which thanks art
The ironworks village
The cleared steelwork
The shelter of lost dreams
The transitional object of memory.

Industrial Clearance

The village has been removed
Brick furnaces lie underground
In refractory darkness, crannogs hide.
Under tidal currents of slag, ancestors lurk,
Factories without meaning appear
Like dirty secrets, land is banked by the outsider.
Development is rapid and hurts,
Vernacular architecture planed flat
With the alacrity of foreign invasion,
Artefacts of history knocked down by
Dealers in speculative folly.

The river grinds out new channels
She washes her town clean
Of your deceitful neglect.
Riverbank and loch, the turning of millwheels
Embracing wall, house and the grind of
Industrial motion, the river ran through us -
Now she spills over in angry displacement
Clearing a new way for power
A topography of wave, the natural
Energy of the work reborn -
In water is hope, in the burn,
We are molecules of belonging
Our energy has returned, renewed.

The Landless League
of Forgotten Factories

The landless league of forgotten factories
Desecrated architecture of the industrial revolution
Breeder of empires and colonial power
The bridges to the past have crumbled
Under the light polluted moon, absence has been filled
With the silent clamour for the unaffordable luxury,
Of history with no memory.

Landless people of the industrial west
Ask Gaelic ancestors of old
To whom does this land belong?
Are you ashamed to claim the soil of yourself?
A clean and necessary job
Lift up the dark shade of the Thatcherite dawn
A sunset of community hopelessness
Draws strength from shoots appearing
In the memory banks of the visionary.

The generation before us remembered themselves
The generation of myself lies on the threshold
Of narrative and ideology, sell out and buyout
Forked tongue inherited displeasure
Internal obedience to the social power
Turning its back on the women, of course.

The land is ours, by use and settlement
Memory and right have currency now
Are we not the people of the nationalised land?
Was it really ours after all?
Cleared away, look to the north,
Track the way to Standing Stone Hill,
Remember the suffering of the glens,
There are answers in wind and water,
Take care, the way is slippery, language
Is distorted, twisted, braid your own truth
Of this I am sure, we are this land.
Do we belong to ourselves?

Serpent Wisdom on the Street

The serpent of wisdom slithers
Up the folds of her grey patina dress
Statuesque form, strong in body,
To carry the wisdom of ancestors.
Daughter of the God of medicine,
Healing temples were erected
In your honour, Athena Hygieia.

The erotic body lies unspoken
Broken in the gutter of the street
Your theology marches onwards
Breaking bones and unborn dream
We do not sip from her bowl
The earth is not quiet
The goddess of health stands before us
Ever-present mystery
A disappearing act of violence.

Art is Panacea, daughter of the universal remedy
The guid Scots doctor honours the oath
Disarms with patience the unelected disease of hatred.
Dr. Walker honoured her, caretaker of our folk,
The weapon is the lotion of non-violence
A salve to the intractable conscience
Touching the earth with hands dirty
With the decay of leaves, a mulch to make anew
The birth of spring, old patterns of fire and moonlight,
The still wisdom of the movement of constellations
The black harbinger of celestial matter
Under a sky teemed wise by ancestors
Shadows stilled by the fluorescent orange
Of the overlit city.

She rests intact in Edina, fenced off to touch
Name unknown, just a place to visit
Schoolteachers are ignorant of her story
The well is closed, water does not flow.
Through the skirts of her marble gown,
The padlock, a chastity belt to the untouchable,
The classical goddess does not fuck
On the streets of Edinburgh, women do not appear
In the memory form of lifeless sculpture.
The town and the city converge in silence
Hygieia does not speak her name
The goddess reminds me she is close -
I know her name
I honour her creator, who loved Burns.
Dearly, she shines on the lovers
Of place-words, silver cups and the speech of women.

Speech Therapy

Unsilencing the words to say it
Unravelling the twisted braids of the confused
Tongues undermining the halting
Speech of the Gaelic learner, unmasking the pain
Of the lost language under the tongue
A field of rising sound, ploughing furrows of vowels.
The consonants sometimes speak
Their silence confuses, an emotional withdrawal
Into unsound structures of hame -
The speech therapy of the learner
Merits praise, dae ye no ken that?

Ye see, I am soundblind tae, word blind
Wi the orthographic confusion o the Scots a speak
In the comfort of the belongin
We were ance pairt o ye, the map o my bit
Is held up in field an river wi the foundation o Gaelic,
Schizoid language mechanisms of old persist
The school voice of the proper
The unwritten silence, the written wrought.
Through tongues wi nae hame in the scheme o things
Never tellin us oor language wiz worth it.

The Jewel in the Crown

I did not sign a treaty of silence,
Words are well, mere words, an early lexicon of mistrust,
We were after all, "the jewel in the crown of the British Steel Industry".
The quine writes of a new republic,
I will wear the Hunterston brooch for a day.
Coila will crown me with the laurel wreath of your name.

Embody Knowledge of the Republic of Hope

I embody knowledge of the republic of hope
A slanting, oblique view of the watercourse of history
The flow, emerging, receding, bounded,
A constant opening of channels, a burn of words
Streaming down from the Ayrshire hills.
Backing us up, a robust defence
For the south-facing valley of seven furnaces
And the winding of the yarn.
Stories woven into women's bodies
Memory retreats of nets of belonging
Nature's mathematical form in furnace hearth
The flowering of firebricks,
Petals from Pitcon, Etna, Dalry -
The mountain of Hephaestos wiz here!
Place-map of forged warmth
From the field of the kings,
Birthplace of my first lover,
I remember the dedication of the red rose.

Classical Blastie ruins, our Parthenon,
Lie crumbled and forlorn under the hammer -
The Ayrshire Yarn Dyeing Company
Dies without respect, the river runs through your shame
We know her power, she is our sound.
The lost objects have been retrieved
Frontiers of meaning gathered in translation
Three tongues of history, a section of the body
John Latham understood her heart
The art of she rises from the moist ground
Flood tide has passed and homes recover
New measures for protection exist
From your source, atone for neglect
The flow of the notation of your life
Simple, practical, already known by us.

We are the folk of the Garnock
Hill, glen, burn, wool, steel,
A valley section, truly ours,
The river pulses, hearts beat to her rhythm
Her veins of water drink from wells of memory
The Clyde will make room for your opening
Northeast to south west, a mirror image of other journeys
Ancestral movements, a familiar pattern.
Template to embodiment, I ripple with your energy -
All flows southwest, the sacred direction of the Gaels.
Goldenberry Hill shimmers with nuclear light,
The Three Sisters are envisioned from the hilltop.

Mothering Movements

Warp frame and winding machine,
Movements of my mother, quick and dextrous,
Fingers untangle knots, skeins of wool
Run through the palm like converging rail lines
Right to left, left to right, a relentless pacing -
A winder's knot binds, an enchantment of the hand
From loose ends an unbreakable flow of wool
Like tributaries of water, the plaid of the sea
The blanket of the valley spinning
with the comforting motion of women.

I shuttle like the bobbin east to west,
Mothering movements of thought,
Words streaming from fingers,
Caressing the skeins of your body
In childhood den of fern, broken brick
Swaddled by the security of water.

The pugs chug on slow-moving grids
Mapping our steel world, contour
Round the water in orbits of history -
Out of sight to human eye,
Secret motion yields knowledge.

The Ayrshire Masque of Learning

In my masque of learning, I am broken-hearted, hopeful Coila
An industrial earthiness hewing lifeblood from soil
Greener now with tilled care, I will ask the smith god
To make anew industrial objects of a visionary future -
The young steps walking empty dereliction
On the main street find no civic pride in decaying statue.
Wordless, children were expected to remain so,
Women, banished still from the clubs of the Bard -
Aphrodite would dance within enclosure of fenced erotic
Mind and open the gates for the lassies to enter -
Hear the muse, brothers, of the backgreen,
Your daughters' mouths and the educated of your ain kind.

I am dear-bought Bess, the unfathered daughter,
Early sociologist of chip shop, café, dyework.
A higher education awaited, society rewarded the poor then,
You did not charge me for the opportunity to learn -
People of Scotland, I invest my interest in your soul
Wholeheartedly, no debts to repay -
Harder to embody the communist spirit, west coast politics,
A radical hairline fracture, red and yellow bilious energies,
Tinges of blue scorn, a barren grey-suited,
Past of laboured indifference.

Black and yellow team colours worn by the new
Breed a new homeopathic alchemy of words
Free from southern neighbours, hopeful
Compensation for the end of the colonial game
I have gone past the adolescence of history
No more mealy-mouthed compromise of power
With the absent father of the absent fathered.

Call time on this dance with devolution -
A staggered reel of dancers spiral north,
Fluid and organic like the tail of a comet.
Did you sabotage us, injure us,
Give us no say, for us just to take it?
Open your eyes to the Oedipal quest.

My soul does not believe your lies, ye see,
At heart who can deny the step dancing of the free -
Covert shadows have less territory to roam
We see the close-up nature of landed power
It was always going to be so.

I am The Star o Rabbie Burns today, coming home
Meeting internal exiles from other regions.
In the inspiring capital of multiple interiors
The army patrol the frontier of the fairytale
The military occupation of birch grove and sacred well
Rests uneasy with the pacifist Blastie, taught by Dick Sneddon
To have hope for the town, "The future is in you."
Underground cupboards store weapons, not hope,
Erase a history named only with faint grey lines
Of charcoal, yet secrets still remain.

In a firepit of burning maps
I am the place of my first kiss
The first crossing of a tear-stained threshold
The door to the steel garden, bronzed in my imagination
A guardian of metal dreams, the loch came
And told you her unkempt story,
The nation-keeping is given to the women's house of workers,
Streets are fashioned with colour, movement trails brush away decay,
All the economic dusting of history cleansed again,
Hard shifts better performed by free people,
The four letter words of human dreaming
So short and easy to say -
Love hope kiss free song -
Need more energy to speak
Wrestle with the labour of naming
Cage, lock and fear,
The pregnancy of a republic, a society of free women,
Will be born through the contracting muscles of time
Every woman knows this.

The Tongue of the Gaelic Learner

The legal mind of the learner lawyer listens,
"How long does it take to build the new language?"
An intuitive question, natural to one
Who prepares a case for the defence,
States evidence for the recovery of language,
Witnessed by our own tongues,
Like the remembered taste of a past love.

"Two years", the teacher replies,
With speed, she understands
The undoing of the English within
Offering a haven for the old sounds
Empathy with due process of time.

The language of the law is embedded
In the groove of my tongue
The throat is in love, offers guttural confidence,
A phlegmatic knowledge of sound love making,
The nose pings wi noise, metallic pang of nasal vowel,
Forged through the outbreath, warm air across inner channel
Nature's satisfaction with her own breathing mirror.

And the sound of I, L for 'luis'
Lingers on the first letter of my name,
Soft, lilting, the meeting point of
Tongue and the alveolar ridge.
Rowanberry, the quickening tree,
Wattles of knowledge hide behind tongues,
I am the letter of the tree of life
In the month of your death
Flame of spirit a red delight to the eye.

As the river licks the shore o the loch
The Tongue tastes the source o the Garnock,
Surging doon our valley, a French kiss o water oan stane
A caress o burn on hill, an orchestra o accents,
Tummels doon the roof o my mouth.
A teemin o voices vibrate, disturb the vocal chords

The nets o language entangle me
Soon the peace treaty o words may sit doon
An voice the fluency o the new speaker.

In her mantle of languages, a blast
O freeform jazzy consonants, feral vowels to exercise muscle,
An open mouth expressive, lips are a safe haven
For your rhythm an probing eloquence
This new language, lusted after,
I take as lover unto me, of belonging
In the body of my mouth, waiting to hear herself speak.

And the urlar, our mournfully pitted ground
Of earth, a breakable coffin of idiomatic structure
New tongues appear, from the mud the water lily floats,
Through water, breaking the surface, an auspicious symbol
Of sound compassion grows, duilleag-bhaite,
A little paper leafboat of language.

Your Mytheology Misses Me

Ah, your mytheology misses me out,
There is not enough vagina in Genesis ye see.
I tell you this merely for you to understand
The deep folds of new life entwined in the vine
Of my muscle, a rebellious period you might say.
In the history of my sex, can you not see
The vagina in the green earth, the breast of that which has
Always existed in the permanent roundness of all.

Hidden songlines of the liminal female, Artemis understood .
Where is the Scottish Dionysus willing us to transform?
Are there no sacred herbs permitted in this land?
Is the frontier of your mind closed to female enquiry?
Doors are kept open, not carved in stone,
They are wet and misty, rooted to the earth,
Sexually free, unbounded by the stern line
Of your stone church and original sin.

I will not be caged in the presbytery of mind
I laugh at your fear of the uncontrollable
What scares you? Are the elders wise?
Is the priest safe with children?
You do not speak on behalf of my sex
The brothers who deny touch
Live in the empty hollow
And dare not speak Desire's name.
I am present next to the nuclear tree
Birch groves covered by cluster bombs
Adornments of metalwork wrought
From the radiated shores of your illusion
Captured behind glass in the museum of the lifeless
Uprooted from the membrane of place.

In the erotic library of the body are leaves
Of unread pages, poems of sex flitting through the hand
Resting for a while in the tune, the vibration of nerve
Willed by the presence of voice, a melody of unity
Chanting a way though tangled reeds
Our landscape an instrument of inherited, passionate ideology.

Black Goddess Loch

The land of the black goddess is female,
The tyranny of the domestic god
Offers the familiar disconnection to truths,
I sense the narrative's repair.

You do not expect a response, praise is withheld
In the emotional genealogy of Scottish men.
Obedience is a tradition laboured under,
Until the work of the unpraising smothers joy.
Your mother never smiled at you, is that it?
Layer the unpraise with unspeak?
Do not fall into a glacier of icy unlove
Shadow box your fears of hate
Into submission on the embossed wallpaper
Of your childhood living rooms.

Violence happened here, no blue plaque records
The enigmatic scars of silenced history -
Uncover for the unseeing eye a lens for the lack of refuge
For the uncomfortable, in feminine Scotland
There is no fatherland in the firepit of myth.

Beside the loch of the black goddess,
In the glen of the great-grandfather,
The land offers the matrilineal exile
Of her narrative, invoke a prayer of compassion
For her hurts remain.

Let my three tongues curl around
The tail of your wisdom
Snaking down the hillside
Clean lines of evergreen like a pubic strip
Line the cleft of the mountain burn
The pain of women held in the falling of water,
the rush of the opening flow, the fluency of tides.

Internal patterns of immigration embody
The history of my women, shame and illegitimacy
Haunting the moving shadows of the ancestors,
Spurred by the workhunt of history, they travelled
To the land of metal and poetry, repeated patterns returned
Of war and sex, the unmarried mother.
New forms of internal exile follow women's shame
As I sit without blame, narratives are repaired here
On the shoreline of Cameron country.
There is no landscape of exile, laugh
As the water flows through your legs,
The valley of the black goddess
Is tributary to the veins of familial secrets.
An initiation of woman, water and knowledge,
This found place, on the shore of Loch Lochy,
Has given me warmth, food and the kindness
Of my turned up, torn up clan, hospitality is welcome
To the grand-daughter disrupting domestic silence.

Dreaming My Ancestors

My dear dead were dancing
They were laughing, imagine that!
Saturn's rings of grief on a dream moon moor
Playing ring a ring a roses, a beloved childhood game.
Laughter offers no guidance, laughter has direction,
The dead danced the rotation of the earth
An anticlockwise revolution of sound
Around astronomy's circles of enchantment.

The circle fractured, a fissure opens to the black world
Submerged in a viscous oil, coal seams ripple through muscle,
Dead matter grows new life, swimming through black suffocation
Of grief, time, it all takes time, Saturn knew this,
Old father issues spiral across ancient space.

Will a Good Samaritan collect me from this ironstone shore?
Who holds out help from the dry ground of Kilbirnie Loch?
The hand reaches with nimble fingers,
Smoothes away the burning scars of historic mines
In hidden coalseams, a dress of tongues licks away
That oh so Scottish black dirt of others' wounds.
They do not belong to me.
I have carried them through vaults and channels of time,
a geology of memory compresses the hallowed ground.

There is no baptism into fresh water
No need for cleansing after all.
Face awakened to the sun,
Naked and bright, wise and still,
Metallic and brave,
This backbone of steel within me
Holds me in water, buoyant and free
Arches in a steel tunnel of grace
Through the bones of my valley.

Psyche sat beside Kilbirnie Loch
Alone, she sifted and sorted the layers
The stratas of human consciousness
Deep in blackband ironstone land, the magnetic
Resonance of our metallic composition.
We hewed from this earth an industry of self
The making of us, the destroyer of us
The impermanence of the steel world
Suffers the limits of extractive knowledge
An ecology of possibility returns to the water
Beside the loch, stillness returns
A transitional state.

A Valley Section

I see the threaded dream
Of farmer, miner,
Steelworker, fisherman,
Lacemaker, woodturner,
Pug driver, nuclear physicist,
Teem and tap, settle and fettle
Whittle and polish, erode and radiate
The garments of your storyline
A magnetic attraction of elements.

Psyche sat by Kilbirnie Loch
Dreamt of her ancestors -

Hard work lies ahead
In the new land, She rests -

The radiant Hygieia will teach her
Of healing, poetry and the art of the smith.

The Architect's Daughter

The local architect was kind to my mother,
Always doing messages she was,
Nae parents ye see, learned to be helpful early,
Wee Betty Gordon.

My name bears witness to his kindness,
Called after the daughter of the one
Who shaped the stone skin of our town,
Art deco splendour still present,
Radio City restored with no interior of memory.

George Smith: Bard

The muse of metal and poetry is in you,
Smithy of the Wee Forge, cast iron man,
Birds whisper to you, flowers speak,
And the names of our world
Are recited in the melody of your rhythm.
You always understood the yearning,
The heartbreaking memory of memory.

We have spoken our words to the wind
Encircling the rolling mill
A surround of thinly planted birch
Our natural amphitheatre, we stand
On steelwork ground, see intangible forms
Well known to the poets of a loved Blastieland.

Your features suggest the traveller
We journey into words, you and I,
Through the woods and beside the loch,
Bluebells, a secret, graves and poems
Follow us, compassion is near,
Sacred herbs abound, wild flowers are glad
To see you nurture the young with tolerance.

A song to honour the musician
The insider's view, an incessant loving
With the satire of the hard-worn life,
You endure George, the town's story is in your eyes
Tears roll over our iron cheeks.
On the shore of Glengarnock Steelworks,
Time has stopped for the poets,
The wind blows, willing to take part
In our lament for the steel valley
You have held us in song.

The Moonhunt of My History

If I came at it round the moonside, new and dark
The silence would remain concealed behind glacial
Mountains of unsaid words, piling up the dead sections
Of rolled history, the forgotten love nets of women,
Shiftworkers moving over terrain, the march of worker people,
Circulating the narrow territories of scheme to factory to the Cross,
Hame again with the messages, quick walkers and slow speakers
Time for a blether doon the street, social knowledge
Usually unspoken, passed on in the icy chill
Of an early spring rising, the cruel sadness of thought,

"Did ye see the bruise on her?"
"Have ye heard their oan strike again !"
"We canna believe whit they tell us."
" It was their ain fault, goin on strike so much."

I will tell my history in the sun, follow earth lit
From the discharging flames of furnaces, a spectacle
Burning the night sky with the timing of the tap
Aerial licks of serpent's tongues shape shifting over roofs
I will follow the light of a smoored steelwork, women's speech
And unfreeze the dormant dead bones of the nameless poor.
Unlit streets of steeltown shine under the gaze of warm eyes,
Looking for ancestors in the stoor bowl of time's stillness,
Derelict stains on the tapestry of steeltown,
Humour helped, for we cared for each other here.

In rooms unscarred by dust, with blazing black-leaded grate
The hearth sun of housework bears the washing line of our worlds,
Warm clothes, drying and mended, clean, simple and re-used,
Foraged furniture and hand me down dishes,
Heirlooms of kindness and necessity, unpretentious
Artists of the home-made rug and improvised carpet,
The humble curtain of privacy an ineffective sound barrier
To the meeting of bodies in wee houses.
Artemis smiled on the girl who kept the silence

Until the moonhunt for words fell upon the fullness of
Womanhood, unconfined by the pause of story,
It was merely temporary, the invisibility.
She appeared on time for the classed scholar
A waxing moon lighting her search under safe stars,
Tools for self-defence found in the bow of time's arrow.

Across the Herring Pond, The Nets

I will follow the nets, our invisible trail lines
Submerged underwater, the muffled voices of women
(never easily heard in the order of the records)
Will sing with Orphic clarity of shift patterns and handmade rugs,
Woven linen from Ulster mills, the Irish sea voyage past,
The boundary mark of Paddy's Milestane,
Northern crossings translate the borders of language.

The fishermen furrow the waves, hands hauling the herring,
Nets tumble overboard and gather the shawl of fish,
Teeming with last chance energy, spasms of wriggling despair,
Across the herring pond our nets trailed across oceans
Spun and knotted, stitched and repaired
By celtic grand-daughters of Ireland,
Belfast Protestant, Highland Gael,
Welsh woman of the valley, Lithuanian Catholic,
The commonality of all compass points of poverty.

The humble fish of the Atlantic follow the hands of the women
Without doctrine, the sea touches the braids of wound history,
Hanks of twine and herring net gather trails of refugees
Following the motion of water to an Ayrshire textile mill,
I catch you standing on pavements of slag,
Memories held in smuggled language and the loss of your name
In the translation of tongues across water.

Industrial Closure

With the pulse beat of the silencer,
The TV psychiatrist intones without irony,
 "It's so important for people to have closure, then they can move on",
For the convenience of the many, please do not remind us of your pain,
Your ineffable link to reality held by a spin of memory,
Open to the freshening of the wound through time,
With heartease, scar tissue softening, fading,
A camouflage of make up the final concealer.

The industrial amputation remains and the phantom pains persist -
The land does not forget itself, denuded of factory -
The steel door is open to the derelict history
Thresholds are not closed to the wandering
Truants of my imagination.

In the market of public space, a privacy of capital
Voices the cost of your extinction
Uneconomic, a regional cast off, a necessary closure -
An inevitable destruction, fated to be strip-searched of assets
The public grief of the people shall be privatised.
Behind language lurks the false conscience of the coloniser,
Convenient for the powerful to move on
Unaffected by grief, no remorse
For the rich man's share shifts terrain
Seeking new enclosures to fence in
The unspeakable profit of collective loss.

The Playing Fields of Class Blame

All bewail the voiced mask of the new puritan
The broken country awakes to the new blame
On the plasma screen of colonial pleasures
My shame is your delight
Platelets for the supply of war
Fodder, fertilised by the decaying bodies
Of the Scottish working class
On poppy fields far from wildflowers
Hackles are raised peacefully
On the myopic red lens of the dreamer.

Disarming facts permit new boundaries of sense
On the common weal of memory
Counting dead factories, soldiers,
National debt, guilt mines
Of subsidised belonging
Pages of the old naming flutter
On a strong breeze, I plant feet
On words detached from playing fields
Without the laughter of women
With furious tongues, lashings of
New sentences for the entitlement
Of decency and voice, classed of course.

Full of accented vowels of protest,
Snapping a disobedience with cool sharp
Mouth spilling your rage
Back to you, across the closed gate
Of the motherless places
Where you learn to order the killings.

There's Nae Tellin

We travelled on expedient journeys,
Quick escape plans forged
In the shadow of burnin furnaces
An blistered haunds,
Wringing oot washin beside a line
A flame penetrating the darkness o this,
Imagining the sighs o a better life,
Away fae here.

Escape plans were cultivated
In the new derelict fields o emptiness
Clods of earth trodden doon by walkers
Trample memories over fledglin daisies
The men keep quiet an till the land o amnesia
Working class stoicism, dinnae mention depression!
Come on, pull yerself thigither!
Go on a wee treat, Benidorm?
Suntanned grief an lager lies
Lyin oan a terrace o exported silence.

Imitations of the cruel wans appear now,
Souls o the communal shrivel
Up against the shrapnel coated sounds
O the landed relics, o the old ways,
Lookin out for each other a fadin fashion
Fear o the unexpected violence
O the dark shadow, terrorisin the innocent.

I huv grown to recognise the language
Abiding in the bruised toon, a second sight
O approaching cruelty, honed
To detect wi feline acuity
The eviscerating snap o deluded power
The keenin o women a radar
Of incomin class hatred, watch carefully
The gaze looks ower yer shoulder, oan the horizon
The land belongs, withered by yer look away.

I hae the writer's hands o the Blastie toon,
Nail varnish red, fire in the mind
Of the well educated, nae callous or swollen fingers,
From the runnin o the threads o time
Textiles beat through the hands o the women
I hae nae bruises fae the man,
"Walked intae a stretcher was the humiliatin defence."
I saw ye move in a choreography o grace
Swift an quick wi the step an tyranny o the windin machines,
Nae tellin o the mournin o place in the gated enclave
Nae tellin o the poverty o expectation,
In the banks o the well fed, entitlement
Is kept in stored vaults, armed wi moneyed reserve,
I weep wild spontaneous love o the
Stripped bare comedy o nothing.

There's nae tellin o this amang the hoarders o riches,
Oor service was in the iron o empire
Rollin out lines of steel, an irony
O language, the unequal angles
O manufactured equality, denial continues.
The speech o the rich is enraged
By the broken, the hurt, the unloved,
The damaged are so much trouble.

Across oak tables o known genealogy
Breakfast bars o modern style
Appearances are kept up
Economies o emotion are contained
Domestic relations are strained,
In the union o the new republic
Fallow fields o silent earth
Grow plants dormant wi desire
A renewal o industry, disarming
Dreaming of natural power
A fair chance for all seeds.

The Sleep of the Seven Furnaces

My voice was rusty with the sleep of the seven furnaces
We bore heavy loads, artillery sharp scrap
Molten guns, toys of male war a becoming bloom
Of a new rolled section across the desert route,
Generals of commerce extracted the wealth of nations
The metal people tilled the fiery ingot flowing capital
Girders of railway lines traverse frontiers far from Kilbirnie
On continents bearing marks of local notation.

Across lines of our making, border crossings of steel
Carry the refugees in cages made by history,
Unfolding the map of colonial time, a palimpsest -
T bars, fishplates, supportive arches,
Glengarnock, a fine brand name we were
On the colonial outpost, deserted by care.

The jewel in the crown tined
In India, Gandhi travelled
Over Glengarnock steel to make peace.

The Last Bloom

The Burden of the furnace cries for release
She has given her last bloom for us,
I wish her the long sleep of the peaceful dead.
You noted her size and date of birth
In the diary I hold with bereft memory.
I place your brass token upon my lips
And write with the eye of the furnace
Glowing upon me, tapping my tongue
Ready to teem the missing script
Of the Daughter of Hephaestos
On the border of a new country
Charging the sleep of the seven furnaces
With the power of Apollo unarmed.

My Body is a Work of Steel

The intricate stitching of unseen scars
Are the undergarments of creativity,
Layers of transparent concealment
Prefiguring the birth of language.

I have overturned the positivist method
Story is after all closer to truth,
History is fiction in the alliance
Of language and power to name
We are close to song in the traces.

Of the last bloom, of our steel
In the care home of the state,
She languished exhausted, silent
Rusty rollers of time crushing metal myths.
I tried to see your beginning
Depict the working class genealogy,
Once upon a time
Was made up to make up
For the unwritten, trust memory
Before authority, of creative origin,
Peer through the telescope to early days
Your stars of coal mine and iron
Forged empires and destroyed towns.
We bore the ambivalence of metal
In magnetic fields of iron belonging.

Defence of The Valley

I have a pugshedful of tears
Stored behind a blind eye, covered over
To keep the vision of the Railbank and the Raws,
Statuesque furnace and pragmatic rolling mill,
Girdered by time, loss blooms fragments
Of half formed dreams, of a landowning republic –
Working souls, power lacking the fuel of poverty
A natural education for the folk
Bidin beside the industry of water.

Cluster bombs bulb underfoot
Radioactive hum over The Three Sisters
Sounds the trumpet call to silence,
The maps of the ministry of defence
Bear no love for homeland
Their music beats to fear, a sadistic drone
Keeping a watch over black night.

In The Heart of My Furnace

In the heart of the furnace
Is the death of my beloved
Unblemished, non-violent,
Gentle MacLeod of the far shore mused,
"I am interested in the age at which
things happen".
You fell alone, a tragedy
of unwitnessed fear was on me.

You died with the ideal eye
Of my childhood on you -
The blast of the furnace, white heat
Love beside you, a vision before you -
A child's hand on your forehead missing
A steelworker tries to resuscitate
The dying heart of your furnace
Already the arteries of brick
Crumble into chambers of dying memory
Blocked valves of history fuzz up the eye.

In the archaeology of my heart
You lie dead surrounded by
The loved eyes teeming wi tears,
Caressing the steel crown of your head.
It is the wish of the loved
Always to be present
At the final breath of the Blastie's tap.

A Am Done wi the Daein

I huv gaithered an soarted
Threeds o ma wheesht wurld,
A am done wi the daein -
A huv fettled the discontent -
An tapped an teemed
Wi the words o ma ain creation.
A hame made red wud Blastie,
Nae tellin an nae rantin
Jist the recitin o grievance
A refusal tae dae the easy thing
An no say onyhing .
Seein a different way o envisionin
The felt textures o sang water
steel an wool,
Haudin me in nets o entanglement
Warpin ma imagination o us,
I have done the daein o the weave,
Combed oot the violence o the clearance,
Tidied up the grun o her greenness,
Tellt stories o oor hairt place,
Rubbed it wi the gentle touch o the beloved,
Fashioned stories o imagined devices,
Enriched ma love o ye a'
Wi the breid o fiction.
I hae kneaded the memories o my ain folk
An listened wi the whispers o the ancestors
Safe aside ye, we endure
Yer industry o history is in me.

The Steelwork Likes
Tae Be Remembered

A hae wrapped maself in a plaid o memory
Cradlin yer water unner ma haun oan the hill
The lang view fae the scheme afore the treeline ends.

A hae sat by ye an poured ingots o grief an lost love
Intae yer bounded coarners
O my map o a sense o belongin
Huggin rusty stains oan a manmade waste.

Ye will ayeways be wi me ye ken
As backdrop tae maself
Ma youth has gone wi yae
Ma een still shine
Wi the sparkle o yer licht in the dimmin shadow
O the work, yer memory disnae haunt
Steel hairts o silent chambers echoin a pulse.

The rhythm o ma words will return tae ye
As source, the water an the metal
Hae built ma mind monumental imaginins
Ma shift will change wi the burden released,
The work likes tae be remembered by me.

Drippin Picture Wurdz Aff Trees

Soggy pages o Dwelly
Hing fae the branches o wisdom soaked oak
Haunds reach up tae grasp the dripping wurdz
Afore the ink dissolves, poolin roon the fallow grun,
Waitin tae bear a broken coffin.

A black branch o the hame o language
Defies the gravity o silence
Haudin doon the echo o the learner's first wurdz,
Fanon sits oan tap o the Gaelic tree
No mindin if we dinnae soun richt
He kens the tongue is seeded wi resistance,
Dwelly in his world hut o Gaelic
Bends the oak doon tae mak it easy
Fur the lassie learner tae speak her way through
Picture wurdz drappin aff trees oot o reach.

Steel Quine

A ken sum o the wummin luk at the educated wan an wonder
'She did her ain thing, disnae huv weans ye ken,
wan o they kind o wummin'.
A hae endured the smirk o the heid yins o the capital,
we know your kind,
A hae pit up wi a the smiles o entitlement of the well- brought up,
Aye we still value manners ye ken, ayeways say oor please an thank yous
Behin camouflage make-up fendin aff conservative cruelty.

They broocht it a' oan an we broocht it a' in,
Tae fester an remove the broken chord o belongin
Tae they seven chimneys o ma steel hame.

Ye wid spen a the money in the rogue last colony
Tae preserve the artifice o entitlement,
Croft, steelwork, mill, mine, playgrun, park,
Scythe doon the weel kent in yer image o improvement.
Dinnae ask the occupied
This isnae a free state, is it?
A things done tae ye, fur ye, no wi ye, never wi ye
Dismembering the hame they never hud
Haudin up the shadow mirror o class.

Fur Me, It Wiz Sculpture

A Blastie Honours Glengarnock Steelwork

Fur me they wur sculpture
Nae kennin how tae say this
Fur we never gie the status o art
Tae oor repeated memories o formation.
A rescued masel fae the tragedy o the unloved
Fae the view through the train windae o the wurk
Oan the tap o bings, hurlin the rid blaze o blame
Doon they gentle, slopin banks
Ahint whaur we used tae play.

A felt awricht seein the big furnace chimneys
Cum at me through the train windae,
The Marxist historian in me kens yer way a lukkin
At worker production an the revolutionary struggle
O the industrial west coast working class.
The traditions o the political left pugle me oot,
Naebody asked the women an weans fur their opinion onywey.

We got aff the train tae see ye
Mak the night sky skinkle
Ower railway sidings stockin art by the pile,
Raws o steel, a heapit stook o angle
An monumental size, ayeways shapeshiftin
An changing form
Maks me think o Serra
Noo I've been tae the art college.
Aye, a ayewiz kent they wur sculpture.

Even tho a ken the grun is fallow noo,
Wi our extracted wealth, the upsurge o metal,
Fae underneath oor feet, a ken a' that,
Wi wisdom heid o Hygieia,

A ken the illness, a ken the poverty,
A ken the wey o metal,
A ken the story,
A ken me.

A miss they chimneys
A miss the wurk
Fur me, it wiz sculpture.